Spar

Winner

of the

Iowa

Poetry

Prize

Poems by KAREN VOLKMAN

Spar

University of Iowa Press

Iowa City

University of Iowa Press, Iowa City 52242
Copyright © 2002 by Karen Volkman
Printed in the United States of America

Design by Richard Hendel

http://www.uiowa.edu/~uipress

The publication of this book was generously supported
by the University of Iowa Foundation.

Printed on acid-free paper

Library of Congress Cataloging-in-Publication Data
Volkman, Karen.
Spar: poems / by Karen Volkman.
p.   cm.—(Iowa poetry prize)
ISBN 0-87745-807-3
I. Title.   II. Series.
PS3572.03947 S63 2002
811'.54—dc21
2001054280

02   03   04   05   06   P   5   4   3   2   1

Contents

Acknowledgments

Amnon Ben-Pazi, Rick Meier, Sharon Mesmer, Alison Woods: thank you. Thanks to the Akademie Schloss Solitude, the Camargo Foundation, the MacDowell Colony, the Millay Colony, and Yaddo for time and space in which to work.

And thanks to the editors of the following journals in which these poems first appeared: *American Letters & Commentary, Black Warrior Review, Boston Book Review, Boston Review, Chelsea, Colorado Review, Columbia, Fence, Harvard Review, Lit, Meanjin, New American Writing, New England Review, New Republic, Paris Review, Partisan Review, Ploughshares, Poetry Review, Post Road,* and *Verse.*

Some of these poems were included in *A Form of Fire,* German translations with English originals, Edition Solitude, 2000.

"Create Desire" appeared in *The KGB Bar Book of Poems,* Star Black and David Lehman, editors, William Morrow & Company, 2000.

"Create Desire," "If it be event," "Shrewd star," and "There comes a time" appeared in *New American Poets: A Bread Loaf Anthology,* Michael Collier, editor, University Press of New England, 2000.

"I won't go in today," "Shrewd star," and "We did things" appeared in *New Young American Poets,* Kevin Prufer, editor, University of Southern Illinois Press, 2000.

"I was watching" appeared in *American Poetry: The Next Generation*, Gerald Costanzo and Jim Daniels, editors, Carnegie Mellon University Press, 2000.

"I have a friend" appeared in *Influence and Mastery*, Stephen Berg, editor, Paul Dry Books, 2001, and received the 1999 Emily Dickinson Award from the Poetry Society of America.

"Heroic Roses" and "If it be event" appeared in the *Second Wordthursdays Reader*, Bertha Rogers, editor, Bright Hill Press, 1999.

"Poem (My hayseed harlequin)" appeared as a broadside printed by the Dia Center for the Arts, New York City, 1998.

We love we know not what, and therefore everything allures us.

—Thomas Traherne

How can anyone claim: "What you by no means know can by no means torment you?" I am not the center of what I know not, and torment has its own knowledge to cover my ignorance.

—Maurice Blanchot

"I always sleep with the knife," said the little robber maiden. "There is no knowing what may happen."

—Hans Christian Andersen

Spar

Create Desire

Someone was searching for a Form of Fire.
Bird-eyed, the wind watched.
Four deer in a blowsy meadow.
As though it were simply random, a stately stare.

What's six and six and two and ten?
Time that my eye ached, my heart shook, why.
Mistaking lime for lemon.
Dressed in cobalt, charcoal, thistle—and control.

If they had more they would need less.
A proposal from the squinting logician.
Seems we are legal, seems we are ill.
Ponderous purpose, are you weather, are you wheel?

Gold with a heart of cinder.
Little blue chip dancing in the light of the loom.
Mistress, May-girl, whom will you kiss?
The death of water is the birth of air.

I won't go in today, I'll stay out today. I won't go home today, instead I'll go to sea. Today is a lot of work, yesterday wiser. Yesterday is a path made out of feet, today is a screwball alarmclock with a mawkish tick. Today offends everyone with nebulous gesture: "I think." "Yes but." "Still really." "Gee well." This becomes language you know becomes destiny, still you know that operator listening in on the phone? She of the darker stare and windy grimace? Yes she is writing every word, I wouldn't leave that blur too conspicuous, knapsack of roar. I wouldn't give just anyone access, but you know best. Seems to me you go out a little too spryly, hardly a step really more of a *sprawl.* You packed your bags reasonably enough, but what about all that dubious baggage from last fall? Seems we're in for shriller weather, your eye no more mild decries tornado and scar. Today needs a few more devotees lacking grace. But yesterday, imperious echo, knows who you are.

Shrewd star, who crudes our naming: you should be flame. Should be everyone's makeshift measure, rife with tending—constellations called *Scatter* or *Spent Memory* or *Crown of Yes* or *Three Maids Slow in Pleasure*. Some days my eyes are green like verdigris, or green like verdant ardor, or like impair. Does it matter the law is a frame to hang your heart in? This *was*. I saw it, schemed it, bled it. I was *then*. Or: I ran with all my leagues of forgotten steps to reach you. A rose said to a rumor, is fame what blooms with flanged petals, or is that cause? Are blind bones brighter in skulled winter or spring-a-dazing? I am asking the most edgeless questions, so words will keep them, so the green gods in my mind will lull and lie. But constellation *Mute Cyclops*, my ravaged child, weeps every eye.

The problem of these Casanovas worsens when they seek redemption.

Is the seducer less a seducer when he is unbodied?

Not desire, but the power to manipulate, aggrieve, overrule, sends these pale boys to hell.

And name it a kinder conquer, when the girls are all frantic rustle and fragrant wrist.

"Amazing . . . you're really open."

Under myopic stars, the roof stoops, the bed leaps: how many more addresses must they send to?

Malleable form, mandible, torso—my beautiful rumor, you're agent, you're gizmo.

I am the moon's lost ember, unearthly pallor.

A tender truant, passing, blows me a kiss on burnt fingers, on fever lips.

"Why are you here all alone? Why don't you go out and play with the others?"

Now I do not love the questions of strangers, which tug close to the loop and haggle in the throat. Yes there are cliffs to climb on, rust and white. Yes there are manyweathered skeletons to startle. But here the liltflowers tilt down livid in the vase, like red cat cries, the sheerest slips of seeing. An all-day, all-waking wideness schools the room, my parent space dryly announcing her long because.

"But you have bones, you can bear them, in any airy ocean, surely the boundaries do not deny you their shy degree."

Or the dark which borders the light's collusive motion.

"But when will you go out and play with the strangers?"

Or when the still shell softly metal mottles me.

If it be event, I go toward and not back. I go tower, not floor. I listen but rarely learn, I take into account occasionally, but more often there are lips to kiss, words to pass from tongue to mouth, white entire. It knows a few names about what I am, it goes door to door saying *She is* or *Her ire*. But when the rainbows are handles I hold dragging earth to more vivid disasters, oh swinging by the strap. You thought she was a dimwit flapper, really she's a chemist with a taste for distress. You thought she came with guarantees, really she's your nightmare hatcheck has a vagrant head. I sort of sometimes go by the book, the need to move being visage, mask you wear like dark sky or water (water that boils or breaks or scares the flame). We don't need a nest to grow in, a bed to sleep. In the clairvoyance of loving wrongly, o glass pillow o swallow, is dream is dare is dagger. Your turn.

Meet me two years earlier in the street. Omega Street. I'll try to be there, to be perfectly present, to get the eyes right. And the rest: the arms and breasts and mouth, the squalid vowels. May they be gathered like frail fruits of summer, terse and woundless.

It's just the early, the earliness of everything . . . it won't amaze me. Precocity of the wrong word falling, bright-blind, the bottom. Bright-early fever of distance. When it hits. If the early, the ago-ness of the error—doesn't *late* me. I will be there, will be accurately other, as right must be. We will agree the street looks better, unbelated. As constellations speak scale to the molecules. A o e

More feet on more legs, more hands on more wrists, more eyes in more . . . Directives fail me, it is safer to bail.

Little skiff, on a sea of excess, it's time your oars struck water, time they moved us. It's time your rudder sent us straiter ways.

Help, there's a sky full of sutures, great gashed heavens of benighted design. There's a mountain of mirrors, and a shore of shattered wares. My ventricle darling, it's mercury's mandate, to bleed and bead and trickle, and stay whole.

Keep me in pieces, I am View and Room. We agents know our affects—plague and pistol—and blur our defects, and shorten our skirts. New ark, who harbors fragments, when your quest is list and languor, will you be ardor? When your dream is blaze and plunder, who will be dove?

May

In May's gaud gown and ruby reckoning
the old saw wind repeats a colder thing.

Says, you are the bluest body I ever seen.
Says, dance that skeletal startle the way I might.

Radius, ulna, a catalogue of flex.
What do you think you're grabbing

with those gray hands? What do you think
you're hunting, cat-mouth creeling

in the mouseless dawn? Pink as meat
in the butcher's tender grip, white as

the opal of a thigh you smut the lie on.
In May's red ruse and smattered ravishings

you one, you two, you three your cruder schemes,
you blanch black lurk and blood the pallid bone

and hum scald need where the body says *I am*
and the rose sighs *Touch me, I am dying*

in the pleatpetal purring of mouthweathered May.

What, I said, noise, I said, is you, are you, all? Yes scream yes shriek yes creel yes bawl. Yes hum, clink, boom, chink, slap, scrape, wail. But is, I said, noise, I said, something to nothing, is noise flight to fall? Is blue noise to black, or scorch to sow? Atom to vacuum, or *Please* to *No*? Riotous wave to staid shoreline? Cardinal to crow?

Or horizon to axis. Or exile to in. Barbarous tongue to *true* language. Me to him.

There comes a time to rusticate the numbers. The way the birds, jug jug, mount in steepleless processions, or the barely comprehensible division of our hands. Or the cliff with the face of a galled god, appalling. And these are boundable, we count them, each and each.

But my zero, windy and sleepless, how to teach it? It speaks to the rain, the spare precipitation—it says, Desert conditions, but I fathom the sea—and rain in its meticulous sermon mumbles back. Talk, talk, in shrill slaps, in strident speculations. As the almond trees flash the gold, precocious blossoms our cold maids call blind psyche. And this was me. I give you my digital, my radial, my baldest baby. While annul! cries the fitful keeper, who sears and scalds. But my zero, sum and province, whole howl, skies the all.

What we know is too full of tremors. An ague takes me like a blade, glancing to futures not mappable as landscape. And you, whom I give my most infinite existence—the dream of a hand and its attendant caress—for this we are quiet, for this we veil our eyes.

Which things will fulfill us? Time's tokens leave their lesions, night and rumor. Ecstasy, to be remembered. A coil of heartbreak in a handshake, a certain sigh. So far, kept hemmed in the instant, of tinny mallets and amnesiac keys—mystic music, love's longing and longing's lees.

Mere predator, do no more leaving. The child bit on the throat will always sing palely, melody sweetened by starlight and dim with harm. It is to *be won* that we wager. Drink the dark dram, lover, and be wine.

Kiss Me Deadly

1.
How do they get so close to the window,
a tree in figment, arithmetic moon?
Summer broke you, winter builds you—
a lofty leafage in the prism, a pure
empire. Where they've ghosted roofs
on the drawings of infants—
because I *did* leave a letter, small map,
semblance. Tarnish the mirrors,
they will not shield. And wound
this ribbon round my fingertip,
to keep you.

2.
Should it be better, going off, grim-
visaged indigents, tinny, mimic stars?
Two things love a third—hosting a harbor
in the brokenest guitar.
Two things leave a remnant—its sound
and space and silence shrill and wide.

3.
Two things torch a fragment.
When did the moon grow an eye?
I speak from a shameless seance,
a blue-lipped winter that mutters and broods.
I move in a blowsy specter,
a gap-toothed slattern with a curse and a cry.

Let's give the lily a scissor.
Let's smash the cup and saucer,
spill the wine.

4.
She moves, she means, she masters.
She deems, she dooms, she stammers.
Schools, and schemes, and skitters,
rumors, raptures, rathers. She *aspires.*
She did, she don't, she daren't.
She shall, she shan't, she shouldn't.
Hooped and looped and latent,
she doth, she loath, she mightn't.
She make, she moan, she silent.
She gave, she grieve, she amn't.
She behave.

5.
Though intentions erode like the moon,
they are still as ghostly, as noble.
Someday to sing it with champagne and sherry,
in a gauze gown, tonic,
stippled with perfume.
An opera of Edens. A synaptic how-come.
In this boomtown boudoir, baby,
you always wrong.

O verb, o void. Not more loose, but I kept a part back. I ogled the hostels, figured the fardels. My importunate frolic kept debtors at a dispatch.

Needing more hell, more harlot. Simple profit. I have a bank-robber heart in a felonious sling-back, and something in a Rubric lipstick would set you up.

Digital spine, maneuver, heart attack. Neon girls are chary, keep their lights on. Blue me a fugue and factor, future mark. It does the drum-roll when our x^2 straddles,

hex of my heart, blight of my thigh,
my heat and light.

Lady of the lake, what does all our weeping lead to? A pair of keys, paucity of summer—just because. I tasted his tears, they were salty, like a seawind—that should have been enough to set sail, acres of stray. Acres of wind-swept granary, what then? Everything blind begins in the darkness. It portends the deliberateness of an unsinking sun, past forgetting, or finishing, the room phrased, phased, like tiny nets of caught. A tree never asked for its stature. So with me. A pearl never counted its pallor as less or more. Why should winds take the pulse of *farther*, slipped along the digits of simple go, of been? No one has thoughts as pale as these—till they bleed them. I doubt more the less I grow, I taste the dark cognition, it is everybody's random. Be your own heart's ending, in the abandonment of seeming—weeping like a two-bit sermon—mistress Sum.

August could ask for better, a hectored meadow, a dross of leaves. Trees are dour in the surfeit side of year, we are speaking purple to the plumes, which smudge in yellow and pallid plaits of flail. The outlines do not hold, the stitched derisions, in summer seepage I am *what* and it is *we*, with my green dress and ticking I am part weed and part machine.

Labor of morning, to lock the darkness in. Where does the night go, Ms. Engine, Mr. Mean? Where's the big-handed washer pures my pie-lipped Rose-of-Rupture, that grow like strident rumor, this smattered year? And the brat of limit with her mottled, filthy fist? This is my letter to losses—swallow *it*

Yellow drapes for the window the sun slits.
Yellow drapes.

Red drapes for the window where the bee lists.
Bee, bee.

Orange peel where my hands held plenty.
Sky and ray.

It's a poem of pure parts, it's already failing, it wants to look at the world the way a bird eats a berry. It resists abrupt ruptures, the perfidious moon, with her shives and hollows and wholeness, gown of flux. What do we know of the flowers, the flashing random meadows, the shy sea cossetting its ruminant tide? The hue and heft of enclosing walls (implied)?

Tender vanishings, that bind a tender scene. Most mist is urged erasure, begetting This. Margin is parent to particle, concealing drape and bright protective rind. So I kill the world when I see you.

Berry, eye.

Although the paths lead into the forest, we are bitter with the bodies of days that end too early. All things tend to a darker dissolution. In a pond, the green flecks adrift, the ducks are dimming, murk preserving rust brine and the fish with a marl fin. We may be guided by grieved grass, the workless, mossy flesh, which tufts the dumb stones in their staunch sleep, awake.

Women who tend the brown days can only listen, it is this that quivers—the no-time, the nothing—which birds have swallowed like lucid beads of sight. If you dig in the earth with your fingers, with your stick, what to do with the blameless accruings? You strike lack. You slap the long oblivion of a blank alive with harm. If it is morning, why are we dying? There used to be so many stories we could sing, the tongue of luck, the dreamwork. And how the days fall like random raindrops, and leave no stain, beside the quiet streams where time is seeping, bone, blame.

There was a stare (yes, was) right here (hope it finds me). Right where the moon blared down its tinny gap. Prevalent predator. Originating— where? Smoke and opal, compressed to a null. Hey orb, what lives in that shell heath, shriek shack? Hey bleach-blink, sheen-gaze, pearl-pith—root of worlds. Splinter in the void's eye, orphan. Got a plan. Got a sea-stitch here in my pocket, like to drop. Limned lozenge. William Tell's pale apple on sable skull. Straggler. Magician's vague lady, hacked in twain. Punk's smooth shiv slid decisive, between the sky's ribs. Waverer, rumor, rock-pit. Pawn, gaud. Vacancy's ambassador, other—we are here.

And when the nights, the May nights, the moan nights, when they come. When they come, the wrong words will follow, glancing sorrow. My idiot Spring, with its hot heart and figures, the flowers lame laws in a weatherbane wind. Where is my silver harrow, my ore-waif strewing pierce-bits with every skip? (In one story, she plays the accordion on the Traumplatz, a tune, a veiny tune, that wouldn't please a monkey.) Where is my inkblot midnight, full of eyes? Yawn, I would say, gall-mouth, fertile fallow: a driblet, a teacup, a chalice, a reeking wave.

And when the morning, the bruise morning, the brine morning, when it *thens*—cracked alphabet of revelation—stitch and line—*then* the foot marries the forward, the fall the toward. Then the null and the next are cousins, in high-noon hammocks of incestuous list. Then what should I do with my waver, my very war, my sky-blue exigency, bloody with minutes? Which extremest west will swallow all this tending?

It could be a bird that says summer, that says gather no late failing harvest in a wealth of arms. Lost weed, still you remember, in a storm-suit, the sky came down to walk among us, oh to talk. Such gray conviction, cracked calculus, chasm. Black earth repeating, I was never him, and so many green words of schism, that and this. If a tree could say, if a tree could say, what are you? to my dim attention, to my wayward random shape. Suit, suit, you're a cold suit, your stitched rain shivers and splinters, what web is this? Unnumbered mesh of other, kill, kiss.

Poem

My hayseed harlequin
what's a bloomer to you

and a bobbin to him?
Two grams of melatonin

won't put the bitch to bed.
—She's mazing in bloody pastures.

—She's got a equinox in the head.
Five six seven eight nine

black angels—ten twelve
fourteen eighteen fare-thee-wells—

won't scrub the slate to static—
won't turn the tone to knell—

kneaded and seeded and gadgeted, well,
it's a why-you-dunnit

and a heck and a hell
and a moon-stung stutter

and a hazy hotel
when a kiss is a vanish

and a flown is a fell.

Or would triumph scathe her multivoweled heart? That none of its eager ecstasy were more than the unctuous augur of a dimmer joy. Opaquely blind, unbeneficent bird of the wisps, stoic as the sea's black silence. So skewedly, dispassionate, one absence destroys its opposite.

So, less than likeness, she swore: the progeny or poverty of Bliss comes this far. To shout it, heretic lesson: that all false hallows have had fathers before them, preceding the grief-arc of anyheaven hope. One promise impotently ends, a finite backward forebear of pleasure. *There will be an equation in the lighter sift of things.* For when the lowest sorrows reveal an odd distinctive grandeur; and the highest, all mind-weals, an earthly outer; or, in one last, a demonic spite and dolor—don't our careless moldings admit the same obscure?

Or this: in the shift of a sad, grass-blinding moon, or hard-hurling, drought-famine sun, one will refuse it. Why the demons are forever forlorn. The many-faced, high-spirit scar in the wing of one, aches more than the crack of reason in the frame.

Octaves, ovations: when some last loop leading the start back shutters and borders and clatters, against your crossing.

Diamond that sparks the flame we are ignoring—in your secretest heart, still—cradle. Activate. Games, like the ones we grew from—tactile, pagan—need void, need volume, auction, to plume our praise.

Adamant ire, in the skull's stem, a morning. Plural keeps and cues me, does me dither. Is what is more than mind is—blossom of a bluebell brandished—when I am?

The first greeting on a bright sift, yes. And the less falls, a loss does. You will not be absent in the day's convocation, as a trickle wakes to find itself in the rift's mind. It drifts from the demurral in the clouds, cast off, to the uniform sameness of soil, a stream patiently distilling itself from stone. A blind culmination, at that trace where nothing stops being, no sweet surfeit—one could reject it, not from conviction, a less rational sorrowing strip from the sky, escaping when the stone falls.

It goes, straying from some refined mass of resistance. Something harder, one height against another, as the gradual, slow nourishment of artifice prevents you, unravelling, destroying no molecule in progress. Somewhere here on the firm ground you have pressed farther apart those ten tricks from the chaos which you rejected one by one—nothing to leave, worth stealing. It never meant to be casually accruing. Under the nothing of what decayed, or some scarcity, staying. Loss implies such rigid divisions. *Come in.*

I was watching for it, everytime watching, for the neck that was bent, for the nape that was bare. The hand holding a cup was holding a thin cup, then the cup was broken, and the fluid gone. So things were the same—eyes stayed blue, limbs retained their curves, slacks and sleeves. Someplace more thoughtless something would happen, less full of couches and women and legs. The windows were waiting, and the lamps, and the hat donned once, discarded, and the hesitant hips, and the whisper which forebore. For all was intent, potential, not fulfill.

I go out sometimes, like a shadowless ghost, less remnant than lip, in the incomparable midnight of intransigent mist, and the doomsayers and lockpickers, cloudlike in clairvoyance. Lad, you keep the latch hanging, keep the curtain drawn. Beyond blue night, when the puppets are sleeping, the stars all coiled in their tremulous wheel, the thin moon summers in my goldenest gaze, awakening dreaming oceans, to drown, to roam.

Sky-eyed scholar, pale Confucius: Put down your book.

Now I promise the shriek that the pressure of days, the pressure of days will be weapon. We drive and we drive, we blare music, we go on. On the highway of our lost intentions, all signs are strident, all exits goodbye.

Who's that voice? A wound in a wheel-spin? Speed—which I love like an orphan, dear dazed infant of my most *present* caress. Lord, I am loving your children, the antic and plastic and plausive, the caustic and restive, the everyway raw.

Think: our limbs are straight, our wings tattered, our tempers *blade*. Still—a starling rustles in your temple, mutant mystic. Still—a something shudders in your fingers, when you sing. That there are—yes, no, then, never—pieces of plan and purpose. That they stay.

When kiss spells contradiction it spills an ocean of open clothes. I gave me to one who hung hearts so high it was a mast in mute blue weather, the clang and strop of it, the undercover wet. Said are they sails your impenetrables that only winds can jibe them, the arc and the rip and the rush of all that flood. But his were slow words, more a storm than a sending, what his hands knew of tack and tumble I will not tell.

If kiss were conquest, were conclusion, I might be true. In the bluebit, heartquit leaping I might be binded. But tongue, lip, lap are brim beginning, a prank of yet. I waxed for a man all hum and hover and stuttered must, what he'd read of snowlight and sunder I'll never pearl. I said, are they moons, that they bleach in your fingers, and so much wrack at the socket, and rune and run. (Like a moon he was sharp when new and blunt when done.)

If kiss were question, were caution. What he knew of. Trice and tender. I'll never. *None.*

Betrayal

A certain
        never said
a seldom
        never would
red Mars
        appropriating eyes
the fugue
        a bauble
to your birthstone
           inflection

more mercury than menace

as I am a flame
        to some
riffing on a purpose
          it needs petals
green-white stem
         "forcing" the bulb
winter prodigy
        yellow marvel
but lacking structure, spine
           why say *wrong*
when you mean *nothing*
         why say *weapon*
when you mean *gain*
        economies
of grievance
        door never closing

the same neck stretched

        like a petal

hello hello

     miracle

claimed like cool water

       frailer bowl

He deciphers my plain lines badly, from whom ideas are not meant to multiply. Such lapses contract or repel the intruder, anemic or shut, an abstained attention. Zephyrs of speed within, freezing; those phantoms which never cease to rave; some industrious zero opened out into a wheel. And later, exhausted with indifferent meaning—a dead limb, a wooden—and the hooks that clamber, implausible hands.

The failing stretches and extends outside it. No more on my tongue was there ever a name. Some instinct claimed a tainting; I saw nothing. My curse not yet growing on my skin, or flicked in the ear like an opulent whip. A thought erected and burnished, boxed in a gleaming, like a head inviting the hawks in. Feet on the voids again, the way a woman might flee, solitude fallen, his cloaked back empty with wounds, he avoids her like a feather.

That was my winter. I ignore the frames. Yes I believed us imaginary/ we did not exist. We could never reason how in the future nothing would not occur, delinquent heathens, refusing to end without a hallow, some doll-faced Tuesday, when it might be free.

Tender feather, tell me a flight thing, never a trap thing, never a fall. From such heights, all eyes are viewless, occluding the warmest winter, the clearest blur. Gold shadow, shell hollow, thread halo—a name. You wondered where the bird was (dear duck, in your arm's own rook, your body's blame). You wondered: was watching *capture*, was seizing *share*? O *thou*, gold thought, unlettered (*there will be blood*).

Yes the red flower affronts a hundred leaves with its brightness, an afternoon's adornment, immaculate device. If the squares of the window, box box, can just survive it, if the world stays perfectpetal quiet, this blank, that height.

2.

Notions, like diamonds, and facets, like very winds.

3.

One two three servants watching.

Which is me?

A story left like prim petals in a pallid bowl. (They were blossoms once, they lapped the furtive water.) Or a story perched on a cat's back, quick as get. (Which came with white paws in our sleep, which came with changed eyes.) A noontime tale, an April-wide, bright sleeper, about the every-eyed field and the wind's aloft elisions and the light heaped corpses of the leaves, the ghostly pages. And the stunned-stump amputations, and the lean limbs, slender rendings, spent, at rest.

What a book of lapsed beginnings! And incipient ends. The greentops nodding in their heights won't think to listen. Only you, old rust-colored measure, who reads in bed.

I never wish to sing again as I used to, when two new eyes could always stain the sea, of tangent worlds, indolent as callows, and the clock went backward for a skip, to rise, to set.

Some will twine grass to fit in a thimble, some will carve bread to mend a craggy wall, some in the slantest midnight cry for sleep. When the pitch-owl swallows the moon, what welt will show it? Sighing helps nothing, raspberries raw and green, in the form of a heart

imperfectly divided. A wave grows sharper close to the shore. Some own words like strips of scape and summon. It is possible to suffer even in the sun. And race the steep noon to its highest, hoary gate. Stares drop under the sky; silence of a windslap; and a scar drifts out of air to stand whistling:

She who listens poorly will always be calling. She who sounds silence drowns with the dumb.

She who cuts her hands off must drink with her tongue.

Dear noon, what goes up and up and never others? What says it's a wind-strung fractal, never whole? This must be some specious season, quick and numbered, pulling the this-world to quivered, hectic ends. Sepals could count it. Pistils, pearly queens. Little godhead stamens, tense, erected. All this *intends*. But sky's blue blushes never meant *o swoon, o love*—o hopeless dizzy heart-song, west of mending.

It was wiser, it kept the mute number—void or grieve. Or where we go, arc-ache of ending, we stay to leave.

Shadow of a Doubt

Link the i to the n and get nothing.
Because I've left a path which knows you.
An indigenous form of blemish, a fatal lend.
Would a postcard in the shape of 2 kisses still get through?
Ice-storms in Spokane left not a tree standing.
Take off the good shoes, put on your boots.
Put your socks on. Take a shower. Comb your hair.
I'm writing to you from a far-off country.
I'm buying blueberries for breakfast, milk for tea.
A nuisance met a notion and begat a noun.
Will you be singing this evening to my green eyes?
Will the mist-mad birches tarnish and persist?
A good day to beat a heart out, to buy a hat.
A good day to fold blue blankets and forget.

The rain falls on the empty town and "The rain falls on the empty town." There are no facts, just cages cross-hatched on a page . . .

If my words for you were skeletal, quiescent, not flat wrecked runes but luminous bones, what animals would grow from these vestigial mazings? If it roars, it's hungry, feed it. If it bleats, cut its heart out, eat it. *If it bleed . . .*

Not that they're lambs or lions, no simple twinnings. No tusk no tooth no tongue says *am enough*, or *sing to the reverend keeper her grim flaying.* A species of three-winged flutter, or pearly paw. Pewter pelt, raw rigging, jarred jawing. Fang and fin.

You lose the world and win a gamey zoo; but won is less than least when I lose you.

Winter Abstract

Call me no one, candle abandoned.
From black lots, black columns, dimensions,
scattering wind. It's been a long time here,
the reflected essences of backyards,
photos freezing in your past. And less. And less.
Wouldn't promise but I swore,
love, adventure,
kept the best of our fractured animus,
when you close the door on your nurture—
cure in ice—the most protected picture
once radical, now quest. Dear heathen,
your magnet is nomad, do not ask
for more malignant fires, benigner poles.

A light says why. From all the poor prying. Again we attain a more regal posture—small bird accompanying slips between our whim. Where will we flicker, loose as two feathers from a wren's back? Gone, do not brood for all the hands that miss you. They hardly hold. Don't wait, one who thought a dark eye could save you, like night with its black paws curled and gone to sleep. There are only two names to remember, *Loss* and *Pleasure*, crossed in this field like no man's borrowed light. Call the far-sighted foxes to the launching. Call the small deer scattered in the back brush, swift as flit. Contingency has arms and hands and wasted faces. And a body, shrunk and scurvy, built to burn.

O coronet—your silver purpose stunts the weeds, the thrashy frays. I won't stall the morning to please you, or give my blanched hands a petal to grip, no strident fruit. Walk downhill, why don't you, or count backward to the fraction that feeds you—nothing to no-one to nameless, to tongue of ash. If substances felt you, fraud, like squalls of nod, if the grassblades pricked their tips to shiny rivets, if the sere-surge of industry were rapture, the *too*, the more: Then in houses, the dust decaying, the fading fades. Night bursts its somber boundaries. The day un-days. "We measure the world by its margins." (So saying ends.)

The end of the day said that was my day. Overnight the field is mown, always attentive. We walk through its callow leavings, *sweep*. Six was more than seven was in those days. An argument for basic enlightenment, for drop. This forest, like a head of horns, a dim migration, June was always increment, stanch, encumbered song. Dirt in a hand like a bird wing. And every palace a ruin. We dig graves the old way, with our fists, black smear beneath the nails to mark the eager workers.

Implorers, connivers, doppelgangers, Uncle Ilya. Haystacks and flowerbeds disheveled by the hens. Old swollen knees and clenched rheumatic fingers.

Of the outside and its perfidies. Taking her clothes off like peeling an egg. The ruined village, where rain seeps through the roofs—stutters on the dented pots. *It rots the heart.* Of what was dug. Of what was silted in the numb, recumbent dust. Of what was planted by sun-slit and cloud-slur. Stitched, begun. The wind stares white-eyed in the field, Aunt Marushka. Space is faceless but it eats us. But it talks. *It has red hands, what made thee.* And *It is always night somewhere* click the indigent clocks.

What I meet of your mind are only artifacts. A scathed museum. And though beguiling to touch what you box and polish, your scurvy treasures—the resplendent ruptures, the dessicated heads—when you splinter to gray mist and grievance, what am I left with? Torques and tremors. Elixirs and whirs.

O bleak elision of the disattending lovers. What furtive dredgings, in the incremental evenings. What slash and scorching amid the tapestries of Then. And *this* was my wealth. Pale capital. This blighted barter. And *this* my beggar's cup, my collar. *All I love.*

And the urge is less than the action. And the whom is less than the when. Been eyeing something in a fraction, that supplants all limits, grounds all pilots, preens, pretends.

A cross between a slave and a subject. Your roar, what I grew an ear for—tremor and debit—and sang gigantic—

and samewise was an infant, and an ingot, and a rend. Famishing, this aperture evening—in the loveless lavish of your scheming, incremental.

As I was saying, nice hat, nice head—a riot heart. A gamine dracula and so much to swindle—the parched, anemic stars, the moon's liquidations. Into this wreck, our valence, our spectral bed—me, you, the astral offal—savoring our lunar liquor, the way we do.

Poem

Black corners of winter, whom
do you pine for?

Yellow broom, sweeper,
who calls you in?

Those aren't horses they're ponies.
They're mules.

Thin and particular,
a saw's way of singing.

A net's way of losing,
an habitual pull.

Eye that is black or brown,
that brims dimension.

Lip that is bit and bruising,
a feral kiss.

Where are you under that red coat,
where can I catch you?

Singing cipher,
the roof is a door.

They make it go, lighting candles, peeling off the rind. I understand little but I listen, I give my fractured attention to the All. Coil of our ire, wanton lasso, we keep bringing the strangest animals home to graze! The farmer tends his arid acre, space between *if* and *when.*

—But I haven't done anything I wanted.

—But I don't have anything to show.

O landscape of skinny lesions, o hopscotch forget-me-not brandished by heathen men, what became of your promises, your oaths, oh where did *they* go? I'm still here—my dubious ticker knows *one thing* about momentum—but in some more saturate sorrow, I am more than carbon or echo: I am fame.

I have a friend. My friend is a sky. There are dark, starved places that do nothing but blur and spend, and the quick sharp blue-black lightning streaks called *punish*. If you wish to do what is known only as "to rest," "to sleep," "to live," you and my friend will have *nothing* to speak of.

He says, Girls fall through holes, occasionally on purpose. He says, Many shapes of web make the rope that will stay you. He says, A bitter metal forms the bit that slits your tongue.

When they ask, What is your friend, that you ash and azure for him? I sing boxless wind in a blanched meadow, scree and scrawl. It is *not* because doors keep the light out, or doom is mortal. It is *not* because dawn calls weather, wander, weigh. If words are wire and can whip him, *this is* the scar.

To take, to make, to message, palled degree. Wood-wend and lesion, decipher. Decree. Candle of warble, shell of rack and pull. Humorless that we do this, old dark and red debt. A room to roam. A wall to fix it. An engine to sing it. A game to accrue.

We should have been so many digits accumulating August storms. And once the little girl slept in streams of her unseemliest futures, a place of plague and puncture and rumored bruise.

"When I get to the hillock, full of germinal and burdock, what lad will have me in my rags? I am the wind's own wastrel, wing and kestrel, oh where are the flames that feed me, mercy's flare?"

Child of the matchstick murmur, the famished lip—

a tune for your tattered tunic, my thieving pearl.

Do not think, beloved, that names greet the known, that needs sheet the night with a plangent sort of greening. It would be more than all we believed if our best skies kept the birds out, and the stars' malignant math shed its incessant drop, divide. Why flawed flat tears, why this crepuscular sighing? Why weirds which plant the palm up, which flack the step? When I am more a man than a motion, it will be icer, it will be *my*, I shall be factored as a statue and twice as stone. But the mutinous falter must flail its flagrant weather, the dry ash wind that sifts the why, and the which, and the gone.

Lost he says nothing. He forgets the blindness. No she is not an ending. He doesn't mean to destroy the least of our spaces. No pairs of wishes and no very few wills, though anyone may use one. There are creatures that cast off a fate in an instant; strangely we save it, it grows clean, mends in the middle, shrinks like a sock discarded after a short nap. He is a spendthrift, intricate animal; I always keep it, always sully it. That's wrong as ever, someone says, and would forget him. We lose it in fields, the open. Finally we dream we have only one, we are thinly an infant. We are used to neglecting worlds. The originals flourished for years, had patches on them, were in no place as thick as rock. And after much, the core is concealed, the skull-stain, and we fall down meaning nothing. And the child, the child, he will rise slightly, sideways in the chest. This will happen in the middle of some callow highway. We will take flight loudly as soon as we see.

Heroic Roses

Because grief's season
is never a new one,
the path strewn
with bootprints, inscriptions,

ice descending around us
like sawdust knocked from
once opulent rafters,
and the lake like the point

in the eye of a lover
reflecting pale parting
and moonlight beguiling
old fear with new fruit.

Then music from somewhere,
myrtle or aether, the rumor
or the cure. I cry
come out, come out, I am waiting

to the same shy pilgrims
crowding the ground:
The mercury bird
is blood-bright in hemlock

for you this morning. The squirrels
do rile the pine tops. The blond owl
straddles the mouse. Or the mouse
finds shelter in your shadow,

palled thornbush, iron canker,
guardian of dimmest
beginning, again, again.
Come out, come out,

I am dreaming
cries one who walks in fissure,
old skeleton, zone of echoes,
when you roam.

No noise subtracts it. It won't leave, or scatter jokes or fathoms, no tiny failing, or some short multitude impossibly, or now, it would certainly never scribble stanched fragments on this less. Noise is not, so words think, a complex logic, no one loses reason fast enough, or then. To murder sound, you must bleed the pastures, the so few animals and vapors, misread the minerals, or still the static the huge stones break when we close at night. You must never dream clouds in coils, convulsive weathers, or those greetings we never felt leaving: nights of adulthood whose boredom is forever explored.

A sorrow not meant for anyone, an ancient beneficence ending so softly, with such shallow and plain sustainings—days in the lavish spaces, nights in the desert, deserts, someone else—or is it too much to never sleep enough, to dream? There must be forebodings of a few dawns of contempt, none the same as any other, premonitions of a few men whispering from pleasure, or of loud leaping boys who have never touched death, and are opening this first time.

I believe there is a song that is stranger than wind, that sips the scald from the telling, toss, toss. In the room I move in, a wrecked boy listened to each sky's erasing, for it was shrill winter, for it was blast and blur. For it was farther from the native birds and the gray heath heather and the uncaressable thighs of the one who shook in violet. Those who fly farthest must always burn the nest. But the mind in its implacable spectrum dims to brown. Must you die on your back like a cheap engine, rust and wrack? In the crevicing days, there are no words for prizing, between the lidless moon and the silver hands of the fountain. But if it is space you must fail in, teach it din.

We did things more dulcet, more marionette. There were equivocations—usual modems—all sorts of agos. Then—in time—the needed accretion.

How much like a star we were, light as blazons. Nomad of a thousand paths, surely there are tempers more like yours, acrid and fulsome, whose articulated measure is a queenly Entire. Then we counted our fingerprinted petals—kept dryer in a pale tin—rose and carnation—loved, attended, tamed.

Be attention, dear border, you wander too far. Your music is dissonant sometimes, calamitous fugues and fallow, echoed tones, you are turning too many melodies into maunder. It seems we are creature, we devour and leave. But when late light turns the leaves gold, when the red pine offers its armfuls of snow, we are not hunger and perjure. In that moment (blemish and blossom) we are *gaze*.

The Iowa Poetry Prize and Edwin Ford Piper Poetry Award Winners

1987
Elton Glaser, *Tropical Depressions*
Michael Pettit, *Cardinal Points*

1988
Bill Knott, *Outremer*
Mary Ruefle, *The Adamant*

1989
Conrad Hilberry, *Sorting the Smoke*
Terese Svoboda, *Laughing Africa*

1990
Philip Dacey, *Night Shift at the Crucifix Factory*
Lynda Hull, *Star Ledger*

1991
Greg Pape, *Sunflower Facing the Sun*
Walter Pavlich, *Running near the End of the World*

1992
Lola Haskins, *Hunger*
Katherine Soniat, *A Shared Life*

1993
Tom Andrews, *The Hemophiliac's Motorcycle*
Michael Heffernan, *Love's Answer*
John Wood, *In Primary Light*

1994
James McKean, *Tree of Heaven*
Bin Ramke, *Massacre of the Innocents*
Ed Roberson, *Voices Cast Out to Talk Us In*

1995
Ralph Burns, *Swamp Candles*
Maureen Seaton, *Furious Cooking*

1996
  Pamela Alexander, *Inland*
  Gary Gildner, *The Bunker in the Parsley Fields*
  John Wood, *The Gates of the Elect Kingdom*
1997
  Brendan Galvin, *Hotel Malabar*
  Leslie Ullman, *Slow Work through Sand*
1998
  Kathleen Peirce, *The Oval Hour*
  Bin Ramke, *Wake*
  Cole Swensen, *Try*
1999
  Larissa Szporluk, *Isolato*
  Liz Waldner, *A Point Is That Which Has No Part*
2000
  Mary Leader, *The Penultimate Suitor*
2001
  Joanna Goodman, *Trace of One*
  Karen Volkman, *Spar*